MARTIAL ARTS, BOXING, AND OTHER COMBAT SPORTS

by Jason Page

CONTENTS

Crabtree Publishing Company
www.crabtreebooks.com

Editor: Robert Walker
Proofreader: Mike Hodge
Acknowledgements: We would like to thank Ian Hodge, Rosalind Beckman, Jackie Gaff, Ben Hubbard and Elizabeth Wiggans for their assistance.
Cartoons by: John Alston
Picture Credits: t = top, b = bottom, l = left, r = right, OFC = outside front cover, OBC = outside back cover, IFC = front cover
Allsport; IFC, 2/3c, 3tr, 7tr, 8tl, 10/11c, 14tl, 14/15c, 16/17b, 18/19c, 22/23c, 23tr, 24bl, 24/25t, 26/27c, 27br, 28bl, 28/29c, 30/31 (main pic), 31tl. Al Behrman/ AP/ PA Photos: 19t. Franck Fife/ AFP/ Getty Images: 12t. Goh Chai Hin/ AFP/ Getty Images: OFC. Reuters/ Steve Marcus: 20/21. Eckehard Schulz/ AP/ PA Photos: 4t. SIPA press; 16/17t. Vandystadt; 6/7c, 8/9c, 12/13c.
Picture research by Image Select

Library and Archives Canada Cataloguing in Publication

Page, Jason
    Martial arts, boxing, and other combat sports / Jason Page.

(The Olympic sports)
Includes index.
ISBN 978-0-7787-4016-2 (bound).--ISBN 978-0-7787-4033-9 (pbk.)

    1. Martial arts--Juvenile literature. 2. Boxing--Juvenile literature. 3. Olympics--Juvenile literature. I. Title. II. Series: Page, Jason. Olympic sports.

GV1101.35.P33 2008   j796.8   C2008-900974-6

Library of Congress Cataloging-in-Publication Data

Page, Jason.
    Martial arts, boxing, and other combat sports / Jason Page.
      p. cm. -- (The Olympic sports)
    Includes index.
    ISBN-13: 978-0-7787-4016-2 (rlb)
    ISBN-10: 0-7787-4016-1 (rlb)
    ISBN-13: 978-0-7787-4033-9 (pb)
    ISBN-10: 0-7787-4033-1 (pb)
    1. Martial arts--Juvenile literature. 2. Boxing--Juvenile literature. 3. Olympics--Juvenile literature. I. Title. II. Series.

GV1101.35.P34 2008
796.8--dc22

    2008004910

Crabtree Publishing Company
www.crabtreebooks.com   1-800-387-7650

Published in Canada
Crabtree Publishing
616 Welland Ave.
St. Catharines, Ontario
L2M 5V6

Published in the United States
Crabtree Publishing
PMB16A
350 Fifth Ave., Suite 3308
New York, NY 10118

COMBAT EVENTS

In the Olympic events described in this book, competitors really have to fight for a medal!

ANCIENT ORIGINS

Combat sports were among the most popular events at the ancient Olympic Games. They included boxing and wrestling matches, as well as a brutal fighting sport called the "pankration." This was a form of hand-to-hand combat in which almost anything was permitted.

Taekwondo

SUPER STATS

15,000 people packed into the Nippon Budokan Hall in Tokyo to watch the finals of the first-ever Olympic judo competition in 1964. It would have taken 307 buses to drive everyone home!

WARNING!

Combat sports are dangerous! Even well-trained athletes can be seriously injured competing in the events shown in this book. Never try to perform a combat technique without expert supervision.

MODERN GAMES

Combat events have been part of the modern Games ever since they began. This picture shows the two heavyweight

Carl Schuhmann (left)

finalists in the Greco-Roman wrestling competition at the first modern Olympics. Carl Schuhmann (GER) went on to defeat Georgis Tsitas (GRE) and win the gold medal.

RECENT EDITIONS

The contact sport taekwondo made its Olympic debut at the 2000 Sydney Games.

OLYMPICS FACT FILE

🎗 The Olympic Games were first held in Olympia, in ancient Greece, around 3,000 years ago. They took place every four years until they were abolished in 393 CE.

🎗 A Frenchman called Pierre de Coubertin (1863–1937) revived the Games, and the first modern Olympics were held in Athens in 1896.

🎗 The modern Games have been held every four years since 1896, except in 1916, 1940 and 1944, due to war. Special 10th-anniversary Games took place in 1906.

🎗 The symbol of the Olympic Games is five interlocking colored rings. Together, they represent the five original continents from which athletes came to compete in the Games.

TEAM EFFORT

Valentina Vezzali (ITA) celebrates winning a gold medal in the women's fencing individual foil competition at the 2004 Olympic Games.

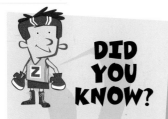

DID YOU KNOW?

♬ After arguing over the result of the Men's team foil event, two fencers at the 1924 Olympics fought a real duel!

♬ The first sword-fighting competitions were held more than 5000 years ago in ancient Japan and Egypt.

♬ Despite being deaf, Ildikó Sagi-Retjö (HUN) proved what an exceptional competitor she was when she won a total of seven medals at five Olympic Games between 1960 and 1976.

The foil has a rectangular blade 35 inches (88.9 cm) long and a small round hand guard.

CHOOSE YOUR WEAPON

You can tell the different swords apart by looking at their hand guards or the shape of their blades.

DUEL PURPOSE

Fencing began as a way of practicing the sword-fighting skills needed for duels. Until the 1800s, arguments between noblemen were often settled by swords or pistols. These duels were sometimes fought to the death!

FENCING: FOIL

There are three different fencing disciplines and each one uses a different sword. First up is the foil.

RULE BOOK: FOIL

Fencers score points by touching their opponents with their swords. In foil events, must aim for their opponent's trunk — hits to the head, arms or legs don't count — and must strike with the tip of the foil, not the side. They can only score a hit with an attacking move; if they hit their opponent while defending themselves, no points are scored.

The épée is the same length as the foil but has a larger hand guard and a triangular blade.

Thesaber has a v-shaped blade 35 inches long (slightly shorter than the others) and a curved hand guard to protect the fencer's knuckles.

SUPER STATS

France has won more fencing medals than any other nation. To date, French fencers have notched 116 medals between them. In second place is Italy with 110, while Hungary comes in third with 82.

FENCING: ÉPÉE

The épée is the modern fencing equivalent of the rapier — a razor-sharp sword that was used in deadly duels!

RULE BOOK: ÉPÉE

In épée events, fencers score a point for hitting any part of their opponent's body; it doesn't matter whether they are attacking or defending themselves at the time. However, as in the foil events, they must strike with the tip, not the side, of the sword.

Fencers must not wear clothes with buckles or straps as these could snag on a sword.

Épée fencing

Fencers wear a padded glove on the hand they use to hold their sword.

LEARN THE LINGO

Get your tongue around some of fencing's technical terms:

Lunge — an attack in which the sword is thrust forward

Touché! — shouted out when one competitor scores a hit

Parry — a defensive stroke to deflect the attacker's sword

Riposte — an attack that follows a defensive move

STARTER'S ORDERS

At the beginning of each bout, the president (umpire) shouts "En garde!" and the two fencers raise their swords. Then he calls out "Allez!" which is the signal to start fighting.

A mask with a metal grill prevents injuries to the fencer's head and face.

MR PRESIDENT

This picture was taken at the Games in 1928. The person standing in the middle is the umpire or "president," who judges each bout. An electronic scoring system was used for the first time at the Olympics in 1936. It automatically detected when one of the competitors scored a hit, making the president's job much easier. All Olympic fencing matches are now scored electronically.

Underneath the jacket is a sturdy vest called a "plastron" which protects the fencer's chest.

Traditionally, fencers wear white clothes.

DRESS CODE

Although fencing swords have blunted tips, they can still cause serious injuries. This is why all competitors wear tough protective clothing.

DID YOU KNOW?

⁇ Even with all of the right safety equipment, fencing is still dangerous. In 1982, one of the reigning Olympic champions died after a sword went through his mask.

⁇ Fencers stand sideways to each other, as this presents a smaller area for their opponent to strike at.

⁇ The épée is the heaviest fencing sword. It weighs up to 1.9 lbs (27 oz) —1.5 times the weight of the foil or saber.

GOLDEN GREAT

Aladár Gerevich (HUN) was the greatest Olympic fencer ever. He won seven gold medals in the saber events, plus a silver and two bronzes between 1932 and 1960. Gerevich is the only person in any sport to win golds in six successive Games.

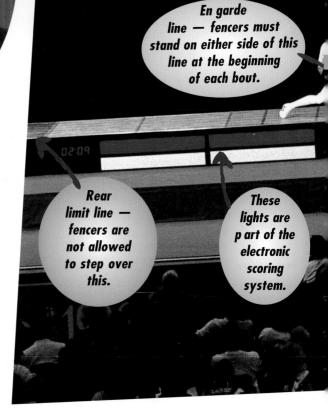

En garde line — fencers must stand on either side of this line at the beginning of each bout.

Rear limit line — fencers are not allowed to step over this.

These lights are p art of the electronic scoring system.

DID YOU KNOW?

‼ Fencers salute each other before a bout by raising the hand guards of their swords up to their chins.

‼ Fencing is one of only five sports that have been part of every single modern Olympic Games.

‼ The gold medal in the men's individual saber was won by a Hungarian fencer at every single Games from 1924 to 1964.

LIGHT WORK

The electronic scoring system uses colored lights to indicate when one fencer has scored a hit against his opponent. A red or green light means that a valid point has been scored. A white light means the blow landed outside of the target area.

FENCING: SABER

he saber events were traditionally for men only, but since the 2004 Games women can compete too.

saber fencing

Warning lines show fencers when they are close to the rear limit.

RULE BOOK – SABER

When fencing with a saber, as in foil events, fencers score points only for attacking moves. However, unlike both the foil and the épée, fencers are allowed to strike with the side, as well as the tip, of a saber.

GET IN LINE

Fencers compete on a narrow mat called a "piste," that is 45 feet (13.7m) long and 7 feet (2.1m) wide; it is marked with a series of line.

ANIMAL OLYMPIANS

The fencing gold at the Animal Olympics goes to the swordfish. Like human fencing champions, the swordfish is very fast, with a top speed of 37 MPH (59.5 km/h). The sword on the front of its head is actually an elongated tooth and it can measure more than a 3 feet (1m) in length!

MARTIAL ARTS

Traditional fighting skills from Far Eastern countries are known as "martial arts." They include two Olympic sports: judo and taekwondo.

MAKING THE GRADE

People who learn judo or taekwondo wear different colored belts to show what grade they have reached.

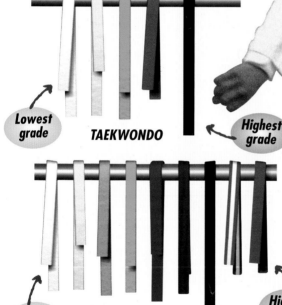

Lowest grade

TAEKWONDO

Highest grade

Lowest grade

JUDO

Highest grade

Taekwondo

ANCIENT INSPIRATION

Judo was invented in 1892 by a Japanese teacher named Dr. Jigoro Kano, four years before the first modern Olympic Games were held. Dr. Kano based judo on an ancient martial art, called "jujitsu," which was practiced by Samurai warriors 1,000 years ago.

BLOW BY BLOW

Taekwondo is a martial art from Korea. Korean, "tae" mean" "punch," "kwon" means "kick" and "do" means "art," so taekwondo" means the art of kicking and punching — which is exactly what it is! Competitors score points by striking their opponent with their hands and feet.

EASY DOES IT

The word "judo" in Japanese means "the gentle way." Some jujitsu techniques can cause serious injuries, but Dr. Kano left all of these aggressive moves out of judo. Punching and kicking are against the rules. Instead, contestants earn points by throwing or holding their opponents on the ground.

DID YOU KNOW?

Judo became an Olympic sport for the first time in 1964, when the Games were held in Tokyo.

There are lots of other martial arts, including karate and aikido (from Japan), kung-fu (from China), escrima (from the Philippines) and pentjak silat (from Malaysia).

Wall paintings found in the 2,000-year-old tomb of a Korean king show people practicing a form of fighting that looks just like taekwondo.

GOING FOR GOLD

Taekwondo was demonstrated at the Olympics in 1988 and 1992, and it became a full Olympic sport at the 2000 Sydney Games. That meant medals could be awarded in the sport for the first time. You can find out more about this sport on pages 16-19.

JUDO

Not surprisingly, Japan has dominated the men's judo events, winning more than twice as many gold medals as any other country.

WEIGHT FOR IT

Fighting sports such as martial arts, wrestling, and boxing are divided into weight categories so that all of the contestants compete against people their own size. There are seven different men's judo events at the Olympics.

GROUND WORK

Here, reigning Olympic champion Keiji Suzuki (JPN) grapples with Charalampos Papaioannou (GRE) at the 2004 Games. Each contestant is trying to get his opponent's shoulders down against the mat. A contestant earns more points the longer he can hold his opponent down; if he holds his opponent down for 30 seconds, he wins the match.

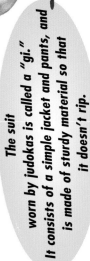

David Douillet (FRA) won the gold medal at both the 1996 and the 2000 Olympics, but was defeated by Keiji Suzuki at the 2004 Games.

The suit worn by judokas is called a "gi." It consists of a simple jacket and pants, and is made of sturdy material so that it doesn't rip.

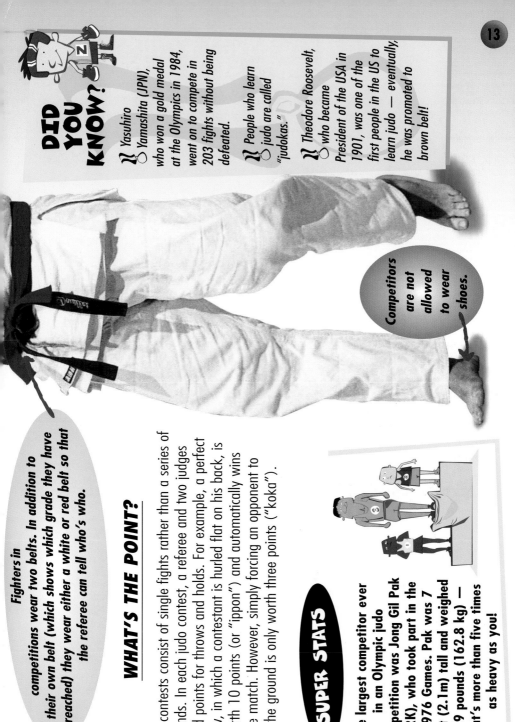

DID YOU KNOW?

- *Yasuhiro Yamashita (JPN), who won a gold medal at the Olympics in 1984, went on to compete in 203 fights without being defeated.*

- *People who learn judo are called "judokas."*

- *Theodore Roosevelt, who became President of the USA in 1901, was one of the first people in the US to learn judo — eventually, he was promoted to brown belt!*

Competitors are not allowed to wear shoes.

Fighters in competitions wear two belts. In addition to their own belt (which shows which grade they have reached) they wear either a white or red belt so that the referee can tell who's who.

WHAT'S THE POINT?

Judo contests consist of single fights rather than a series of rounds. In each judo contest, a referee and two judges award points for throws and holds. For example, a perfect throw, in which a contestant is hurled flat on his back, is worth 10 points (or "ippon") and automatically wins the match. However, simply forcing an opponent to the ground is only worth three points ("koka").

SUPER STATS

The largest competitor ever in an Olympic judo competition was Jong Gil Pak (PRK), who took part in the 1976 Games. Pak was 7 feet (2.1m) tall and weighed 359 pounds (162.8 kg) — that's more than five times as heavy as you!

lightweight (73 kg): Lee Won-Hee (KOR) / half-middleweight (81 kg): Ilias Iliadis (GRE) / middleweight (90 kg): Zurab Zviadauri (GEO) half-heavyweight (100 kg): Igor Makarau (BLR) / heavyweight (over 100 kg): Keiji Suzuki (JPN)

JUDO (CONTINUED)

Women competed in judo events for the first time in 1992. There are now seven weight classes for women — the same number as for men.

Marie-Claire Restoux (FRA) struggles underneath an opponent at the 1996 Games

GIVE UP YET?

Armlocks and strangleholds can be used to force an opponent to submit. If a competitor cannot get out of a hold, he can surrender by tapping the mat several times with his hand.

LEARN THE LINGO

Judo's technical terms are all in Japanese.

Dojo — a training hall
Hajime — begin fighting
Rei — bow
Sore-made — the contest is over
Senshu — a judo champion

THE BIG BANG

When contestants are thrown during a judo contest, they usually hit the mat with a loud bang. However, it's not nearly as painful as it sounds! In fact, the noise is made by competitors slapping their arm against the mat. This technique breaks their fall and actually prevents serious injuries.

NICE THROW

Ryoko Tamura (JPN) throws Kye Sun (PRK) during the women's extra-lightweight final at the 1996 Olympic Games. Tamura was beaten into second place at Atlanta, but then came back to win gold at both the 2000 and the 2004 Games. She has also won the women's lightweight world championship seven times!

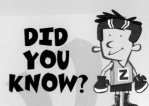

DID YOU KNOW?

Before each judo match begins, the contestants bow to the referee and each other as a sign of respect.

Tamura's defeat at the 1996 Games was her first defeat in 84 matches.

Judo is the only Olympic sport in which competitors are allowed to break each other's arms!

BATTLE ZONE

Competitors must stay inside the contest area when they are fighting. The contest area is covered by a firm rubber mat, and is surrounded by a red border to warn the competitors when they are getting too close to the edge.

lightweight (57 kg): Yvonne Bönisch (GER) / half-middleweight (63 kg): Ayumi Tanimoto (JPN) / middleweight (70 kg): Masae Ueno (JPN) / half-heavyweight (78 kg): Noriko Anno (JPN) / heavyweight (over 78 kg): Maki Tsukada (JPN)

SMASHING TIME

A traditional part of taekwondo training is called "kyukpa," which means "breaking." This involves smashing planks of wood, tiles and even bricks, using only the body — fists, elbows, feet, and hands. Kyukpa is not done just to impress. It is an important practice technique and a way of testing precision and power. It takes years to master — don't be tempted to try it at home!

Taekwondo: kyukpa

DID YOU KNOW?

There are four different weight categories in the Olympic taekwondo competition.

A contestant is automatically disqualified if he is given three penalty points.

Each taekwondo contest is made up of three rounds (called "jeons") and each round lasts for 3 minutes.

JOO WHO?

"Joo-sim" is the name given to the referees. They are assisted by four judges — one on each corner of the fighting area. The judges award the contestants a point every time they land a legal blow on their opponents, and deduct a point for each foul they commit.

Starting a taekwondo contest

TAEKWONDO

Competitors from North and South Korea are at the top of the Men's Olympic taekwondo league, winning four medals across both the 2000 and 2004 Games.

RULE BOOK

In taekwondo, contestants are allowed to attack only the front part of their opponents' bodies, and can only use punches and kicks — the throws used in judo, for example, are strictly forbidden. All punches must be above the waist and kicks are allowed only when attacking the opponent's head.

SUPER STATS

STARTER'S ORDERS

At the start of a taekwondo contest, the referee shouts "cha-ryeot," the command for both contestants to stand to attention. When the referee shouts "kyeong-rye," both contestants bow. Finally, the referee shouts out "shi-jak!" which is the signal to start fighting.

Taekwondo is now practiced by around 40 million people in 142 different countries all over the world. If everyone who did taekwondo joined hands, they could form a line that would stretch around the middle of Earth 1.25 times!

welterweight (80 kg): Steven Lopez (USA) /
heavyweight (over 80 kg): Dae-Sung Moon (KOR)

TAEKWONDO
(CONTINUED)

With four women's weight categories in the taekwondo events, it's not just the men who pack a punch at the Olympics!

Pads must be worn under the dubok to protect the competitor's shins, groin and forearms.

COLOR CODE

To help the referee identify the competitors, contestants have different colored markings on their body pads — one wears red ("hong"), the other wears blue ("chung"). These markings also show the three target areas on a competitor's body that his opponent must aim for. Blows outside of these areas (apart from blows to the head) incur penalties.

A padded body guard is worn over the chest to soften kicks and punches.

Taekwondo competitors

LEARN THE LINGO

A quick guide to some more of taekwondo's tricky terminology:

Dung-joomock chi-gi
— back-fist punch

Sob-nal chi-gi — knife-hand punch

Palkoop chi-gi — elbow punch

Dwi cha-gi — back kick

Yop cha-gi — side kick

QUICK THINKING

Fighting sports such as taekwondo aren't just about attacking your opponent. They are also about defending yourself — and competitors need lightning-quick reflexes! In this picture, Luo Wei (CHN), welterweight champion, fights Hwang Kyung Sun (KOR).

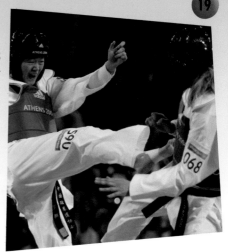

Colored markings identify each competitor and mark out target areas for hitting.

PENALTY POINTS

Grabbing, pushing, or tripping an opponent is against the rules and results in a penalty point. The same applies when a contestant deliberately steps outside of the contest area on the mat or turns his back towards his opponent.

The white suit worn by the competitors is known as a "dubok." It is made of a lighter material than the suit worn in judo.

DID YOU KNOW?

Around 100 competitors will be competing for gold medals at the 2008 Beijing Olympics.

As in boxing, if a contestant is knocked down and does not get up within 8 seconds, his opponent automatically wins the contest.

Unlike most Olympic events, two bronze medals are awarded in taekwondo, judo, and boxing.

welterweight (67 kg): Luo Wei (CHN) /
heavyweight (over 67 kg): Chen Zhong (CHN)

DID YOU KNOW?

❓ Boxing events were not held at the Olympics in 1912 because the sport was against the law in Sweden, which is where the Games were held that year!

❓ At the beginning of a match, the two competitors shake hands by touching their gloves together.

❓ At the 1996 Olympic Games, Cuban boxers won gold or silver medals in 7 out of the 12 events!

HANDS UP!

At the end of a match, both boxers stand in the center of the ring, one on either side of the referee. The referee then raises the winner's arm up into the air to show the spectators who has won. Here, Thailand's Worapoj Petchkoom falls to his knees after losing the bantamweight gold medal to Cuba's Guillermo Rigondeaux Ortiz (in the background) at the 2004 Athens Games.

WEIGH TO GO

There are 12 Olympic boxing events. Boxers fight in the event that is appropriate to their weight. This chart shows the maximum weight for each event.

BOXING WEIGHT CATEGORIES

Light-flyweight: 48 kg/106 lb	Flyweight: 51 kg/112 lb
Bantamweight: 54 kg/119 lb	Featherweight: 57 kg/126 lb
Lightweight: 60 kg/132 lb	Light-welterweight: 63.5 kg/140 lb
Welterweight: 67 kg/148 lb	Light-middleweight: 71 kg/157 lb
Middleweight: 75 kg/165 lb	Light-heavyweight: 81 kg/179 lb
Heavyweight: 91 kg/201 lb	Super-heavyweight: over 91 kg/201 lb

REIGNING OLYMPIC CHAMPIONS: **Light-flyweight:** Yan Barthelemy (CUB) / **flyweight:** Yuriorkis Gamboa (CUB)

BOXING

The first recorded boxing event at the ancient Olympic Games took place in 688 BCE. The contestants wrapped strips of leather around their hands and fought each other until one competitor was knocked unconscious!

CLOSE SHAVE

There are strict rules about who can take part in boxing events at the modern Olympics. For a start, all competitors must be men — there are no Olympic boxing events for women. Boxers must also be over 17 years old but under 34, for health reasons. Another rule says that competitors can't compete if they have beards!

GIVE US A RING

Boxing matches take place in what's called a "ring," although it's actually square in shape! The ring is surrounded by four elastic ropes and each side is over 20 feet (6.1m) long. The corners of the ring are colored: one is red, one is blue (one for each opponent), while the other two are white (neutral).

It's not just humans who like to box — kangaroos do it too! Young kangaroos often play at boxing each other with their front paws. However, you wouldn't want to get into a real fight with a kangaroo, as a blow from one of its back legs is powerful enough to kill.

ANIMAL OLYMPIANS

BOXING (CONTINUED)

The modern rules of boxing are based on the "Queensbury rules," which drawn up in the 1800s. One rule was that all boxers should wear proper leather gloves!

Boxing rules

BUTTON IT!

Olympic boxing matches are scored by a panel of five judges using an electronic scoring system. Each judge has two buttons in front of him, one for each boxer. Each time a boxer has scored a point, the judges press the appropriate buttons. However, the boxer doesn't get the point unless at least two of the judges agree.

In Olympic events all boxers must wear protective headgear.

Professional boxers fight bare chested, but Olympic boxers must wear sleeveless vests when competing.

SUPER STATS

The USA is the most successful boxing nation. From 19 Games, they have produced 48 Olympic champions. Cuba is second with 30 gold medals, while the former Soviet Union and Italy are tied for third place with 14.

Long lace-up boots support boxers' ankles and help them grip the mat.

László Papp (HUN)

Boxers wear padded gloves. Inside, their hands are wrapped in bandages for added protection.

TRIPLE GOLD TRIUMPH

IN 1956, Lázló Papp (HUN) became the first boxer ever to win three Olympic gold medals. This feat was equaled by Teofilio Stevenson (CUB) in 1980. At the Sydney Games, Cuban Felix Savon attempted to win his third Olympic victory in a row, but was defeated.

Boxers' shorts must have a clear "beltline." If their opponent hits them below this, it is counted as a foul.

A DIRECT HIT

The judges only award a point to a boxer if he hit his opponent on the front or side of the torso, or the front or side of the head. Blows to his opponent's arms don't count. To be valid, a punch must be made with the knuckles of the glove and, in the judges' opinion, be powerful. Blows with no force behind them don't count.

DID YOU KNOW?

Boxing is probably the most dangerous of all Olympic sports and some people believe it should be banned.

Three doctors are required to attend every Olympic fight.

In 1908, Reg Baker (AUS) made it to the final of the Olympic middleweight contest — not bad considering he was also a member of the Australian swimming and diving teams!

DID YOU KNOW?

🥊 The ancient Greeks had their own Olympic boxing heroes too — men such as Theagenes from Thasos, who won the boxing event almost 2,500 years ago in 480 BCE.

🥊 The referee shouts "seconds away" before the start of each round to tell the seconds (see right) to get out of the ring.

🥊 If a coach wants to stop the fight and withdraw his boxer, he simply throws a towel into the ring.

BREATHING SPACE

Between rounds, the boxers return to their corners and are allowed one minute's rest. During this time, their coaches and 'seconds' (the coaches' assistants) are allowed to give them advice and tend to minor injuries. Here, the four-time world heavyweight champion, Felix Savon (CUB), takes a rest.

Cassius Clay (USA)

BIG HITS

Boxing champions such as George Foreman (USA), Joe Frazier (USA) and Lennox Lewis (CAN) were all Olympic gold medalists. The famous Cassius Clay (also known as Muhammad Ali) is seen here with his gold medal in 1960.

BOXING
(CONTINUED)

Many boxers won gold medals at the Olympics before achieving even greater success and fame as professional boxers.

ALL CHANGE

Previously, Olympic boxing matches consisted of three rounds lasting 3 minutes each. For 2008 Beijing Games, this has been changed to five 2-minute rounds. The beginning and end of each round is signaled by the ringing of a bell.

LEARN THE LINGO

These boxing terms are a knockout!

Lead arm — the arm that the boxer uses to jab his opponent

Jab — a short, quick punch

Southpaws — a left-handed boxer who jabs with his right arm

Sparring — practice fights

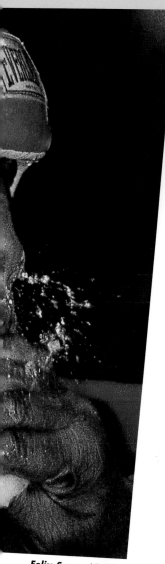

Felix Savon (CUB)

AND THE WINNER IS...

Boxers can win an Olympic boxing match by scoring more points than their opponents, or by a "knockout" — when a boxer knocks down his opponent, who is then unable to get up within 10 seconds (as counted by the referee). A competitor can also withdraw from the match, or be withdrawn by the referee or his own coach. And boxers can be disqualified for committing a foul!

heavyweight: Odlanier Solis (CUB) / **super-heavyweight**: Aleksandr Povetkin (RUS)

WRESTLING

There are two different wrestling disciplines — Greco-Roman and freestyle — with seven events in each.

The same mat is used in both forms of wrestling. The mat is at least 2 inches (5.1 cm) thick and is raised off the ground to give spectators a better view.

RULE BOOK

In both Greco-Roman and freestyle wrestling, competitors are awarded points for throws and holds performed on their opponents; whoever has the most points at the end of the match wins. A wrestler can also win by opening up a 10-point lead or managing to pin his opponent's shoulder blades against the floor for half a second.

The "safety zone" is colored blue and must be at least 5 feet (1.5m) wide. The wrestlers may not cross into this zone.

The "central circle" is a small yellow ring in the middle of the mat where the wrestlers start each bout.

Soviet Union	68
USA	52

SUPER STATS

Competitors from the former Soviet Union have won 68 victories in wrestling events. The USA comes second with 52 victories, although it has only won five golds in the Greco-Roman events.

Weight categories for men's freestyle wrestling: -55 kg, 55 - 60 kg, 60 - 66 kg, 66 - 74 kg, 74 kg - 84 kg, 84 - 96 kg, 96 - 120 kg.

The "passivity zone" is a red border about 3 feet (0.9m) thick which shows the wrestlers that they are approaching the edge of the mat.

NO LEGS!

In Greco-Roman wrestling, unlike freestyle wrestling, competitors are not allowed to attack their opponent's legs or use their own legs to attack.

DID YOU KNOW?

〽 Only two people have won a gold medal in both wrestling styles at the same Games.

〽 The most medals ever won by a wrestler is five. Wilfred Dietrich (GER) won one gold, two silvers and two bronzes between 1956 and 1968.

〽 Wrestling used to be a men-only event, but in 2004, a women's category was introduced.

The 'central wrestling area', where most of the action takes place, is Colored yellow and is 23 feet wide.

Wrestling mat

TIME FOR CHANGE

Modern wrestling bouts consist of two 3-minute rounds, with 3 minutes of extra time in the event of a draw. However, until 1924, competitions had no time limits. In 1912, Martin Klein (RUS) and Alfred Asikáinen (FIN) wrestled for 11 hours and 40 minutes. Klein eventually won but was too exhausted to compete in the final!

Martin Klein & Alfred Asikáinen

Categories for women's freestyle wrestling: -48 kg, 48 - 55 kg, 55 - 63 kg, 63 - 72 kg.

DID YOU KNOW?

Only one Greek competitor has won a gold medal in Greco-Roman wrestling!

The greatest wrestler in ancient times was a man known as Milon of Croton who won five Olympic golds between 532 and 516 BCE.

In ancient times, wrestlers were allowed to rub oil on their bodies to make their skin slippery. This is forbidden in modern wrestling contests.

BUILDING A BRIDGE

One of the classic defensive moves in Greco-Roman wrestling is known as the "bridge" and it requires great strength. In this move, the wrestler arches his back and balances on his head and toes to stop his opponent pinning his shoulders to the ground. Pasquale Passarelli (FRG), in the bantamweight final in 1984, managed to hold this position for 96 seconds and won the gold medal.

Yuriy Melnichenko (KAZ) & Denis Hall (USA)

WANT A LIFT?

Three time Olympic gold medalist Alexandr Karelin (RUS), left, is seen here fighting Siamak Ghaffar (USA) at the 1996 Olympics. Karelin is one of the strongest men ever to compete at the Games. He specializes in a move known as the "Karelin Lift," in which he picks up opponents and throws them over his head!

GRECO-ROMAN WRESTLING

Lifts, throws, tumbles, and turns — it's hard to keep your feet on the ground when you're a Greco-Roman wrestler!

RULE BOOK

Wrestlers are awarded one point for a "take down" (forcing an opponent down on to the mat); two points for turning an opponent over so that his back is on the mat; three points for taking an opponent off his feet and turning him over all in one move; and five points for throwing an opponent in the air.

Check out these traditional wrestling terms:

LEARN THE LINGO

Fall — pinning the opponent's shoulders to the ground.

Tomber — this is the French word for "fall." If a wrestler can hold his opponent's shoulder's down for as long as it takes the referee to say "tomber" (1 second), he wins the match.

Take down — overpowering the opponent and gradually forcing him to the ground.

KEEP A HANKY HANDY

One of the more unusual wrestling rules says that all competitors in Greco-Roman events must have a handkerchief tucked into their clothing! This dates back to the time when wrestlers had to wipe blood or sweat off of their bodies — now wrestlers use antiseptic sprays.

FREESTYLE WRESTLING

If you like wrestling that's fast and furious, then you'll love freestyle!

FAIR GAMES

Freestyle wrestling became popular in Britain and the USA during the 1800s because it's faster and more dramatic than the traditional Greco-Roman style. Known as "catch as catch can," freestyle contests were often held at fairs and festivals. Freestyle events were held at the Olympic Games for the first time in 1904.

SUPER STATS

The heaviest competitor in Olympic history was a freestyle wrestler named Chris Taylor (USA), who won a bronze medal at the Games in 1972. Taylor weighed 419 pounds — that's almost twice as heavy as most adults!

Townsend Saunders (USA) & Vadim Bogiyev (RUS)

LEG IT!

Grabbing an opponent's legs, as the wrestler wearing red is doing in this picture, is permitted in freestyle contests. Tripping an opponent or holding him with the legs is also allowed.

One wrestler wears red and the other wears blue, to help the referee identify them.

RULE BOOK

In a wrestling match, competitors are not allowed to pull their opponent's hair or ears, twist their fingers or touch their faces. Biting, pinching, kicking, punching, and striking with the elbow are also forbidden, as is holding on to an opponent by his clothes.

DID YOU KNOW?

In 1980, the Beloglazov twins (URS) both won gold medals in the freestyle. At the 1984 Games, the Schultz twins (USA) repeated the feat!

In 1904, all seven freestyle events were won by wrestlers from the USA — the only country that entered the competition!

Wrestlers are not allowed to talk to each other during a bout.

INDEX

COUNTRY ABBREVIATIONS

ALG – Algeria
AUS – Australia
AZE – Republic of Azerbaijani
BUL – Bulgaria
CAN – Canada
CHN – China
CUB – Cuba
EGY – Egypt
FIN – Finland
FRA – France
FRG – West Germany (1949-90)
GER – Germany
GRE – Greece
HUN – Hungary
IRI – Iran
ITA – Italy
JPN – Japan

KAZ – Kazakhstan
KOR – Korea
POL – Poland
PRK – Democratic People's Republic of Korea
ROM – Romania
RUS – Russia
SUI – Switzerland
THA – Thailand
TUR – Turkey
TPE – Chinese Taipei
UKR – Ukraine
URS – Soviet Union (1922-92)
USA – United States of America
UZB – Republic of Uzbekistan